Self-Discipl
Beginners

The Ultimate Guide to Achieve goals, Willpower, Motivation & powerful Habits. Learn Self-Discipline, Stress Management, and avoid procrastination.

Written By

James Foster

Table of Contents

INTRODUCTION 7

TUNE IN THEIR CURRENT MOOD STATES 9

HABITS OF PEOPLE WITH REMARKABLE MENTAL TOUGHNESS 17

OVERTHINKING AND MENTAL TOUGHNESS.................................... 25

HOW TO BE A HIGHLY SENSITIVE PERSON (HSP).......................... 43

HIGH SENSITIVY AND HIGH SENSATION SEEKING 61

SELF-DISCIPLINE ON EMPATHY.................................... 69

IMPORTANCE OF OOPTIMAL AROUSAL LEVEL 77

FIND YOURSELF AND FORGETTING STEROTYPES (EMPATH HEALING) 97

BIOLOGICAL STRANGENESS.................................... 101

HOW DIFFERENT ARE WE REALLY?........................... 105

CONCLUSION 113

INTRODUCTION

Thank you for purchasing this book!

Why does mental toughness matter so much? And how do you plan to develop more?

Now let us define and discuss it. Mental toughness could be defined in various ways, which are below.

Academic definition for Mental Toughness:

"Mental toughness is the ability to resist, manage, and overcome doubts, panics, concerns, and circumstances that prevent you from succeeding or excelling in a task or towards a goal or performance outcome that you are set to achieve."

Sport psychology definition for Mental Toughness:

In Sport Psychology, the term 'mental toughness' has long been used. I got familiar with mental toughness in sport, soccer to be precise, watching the likes of Cristiano Ronaldo and Lionel Messi, both dominating the world of football for over a decade now. I am forced to say these two men are very mentally tough. We might never have these men in the history of football again.

Definition: "Having the natural or developed psychological edge that allows you to: generally, cope better than your opponents with the many demands (competition, training, lifestyle) that sport places on a performer; in particular, be more consistent and better than your opponents in remaining resolute, focused, confident and under pressure."

What distinguishes mental toughness from the core?

Mental toughness skills are an advantage to possess in all areas of life. Those who practice and own the attribute that we call "mental toughness" quickly ascend to positions of authority and leadership in industry, sports, show business, besides excelling in their personal lives.

Enjoy your reading!

TUNE IN THEIR CURRENT MOOD STATES

The best way to interpret it is in terms of emotional reactivity for all the talk of the Emotional Quotient as "intelligence."

Think of that ranging from Steve Jobs and Woody Allen on one end (low Emotional Quotient / high reactivity) to the Queen of England, and Angela Merkel on the other (high Emotional Quotient / low reactivity).

Mood swings in people with lower Emotional Quotient are rising behavioral currency but this is at least predictable. What's the Change of Mood?

"Mood swings" is a common term used to describe emotions which fluctuate rapidly and intensely. We also describe mood swings as a "roller coaster" of emotions ranging from happiness and satisfaction to frustration, irritability, and even depression.

A person may notice something in their mood that has "triggered" a change, such as a stressful event at work.

But it's also not unusual for there to be mood swings without an obvious cause. Over the course of a day or even within a few hours, people may experience these changes in mood.

For example, your grumpy coworker might say that when they arrive at the office they feel irritable, they "wake up on the wrong side of the bed." If you see them later in the day they may have changed their mood. In reality, they may not even remember why they were previously in a bad mood.

What are the reasons behind Mood Swing?

Everyone experiences mood swings from time to time, but if you seem to get them frequently or they're so serious that they interrupt your everyday life (including work and relationships), this may be a symptom of an underlying condition needing medication.

Internal changes that take place in our lives affect our mood, but it's not just what's going on inside that defines how we feel; we respond to what's going on around us, too. Our emotions can also be affected by external changes in our lives and environments, such as increased stress at home, school or work.

1.   Illness and injury: Although the word "mood swings" suggests an emotional cause, the changes may also be associated with chronic diseases or acute brain injuries, such as dementia, coma, or a stroke. Other medical conditions (especially neurological conditions) may also cause swings in mood, including diabetes, sleep disorders, multiple sclerosis, thyroid disorders, Parkinson's disease.

2.   Developmental: Toddlers and young children frequently become "moody" as they learn to control their feelings, and may throw tantrums. Although they are usually a normal part of emotional development, children's mood swings can also be a symptom of an underlying mental health disorder, learning disability, or even a physical condition. Children and adolescents with attention deficit hyperactivity disorder, for example, may experience mood shifts that may interfere with school and friendships. As children get older, the mood swings remain a natural part of their development. By the time you reach the

preteen years, mood swings are driven primarily by hormonal changes. These mood shifts tend to peak during puberty and stabilize slowly by young adulthood.

3.   Diet: A person who is eating a diet that's nutritionally inadequate or not getting enough to eat may experience mood changes in response to fluctuating blood sugar levels and malnourishment. For example, if you notice your grouchy coworker has more spring in their step after they have breakfast and a cup of coffee, their bad morning mood may have been stemming from caffeine withdrawal or low blood sugar (hypoglycemia).

Digestive disorders that affect the body's ability to absorb nutrients, such as Celiac disease and inflammatory bowel disease (IBD), have also been associated with mood swings. These conditions have also been linked to specific mental health conditions, such as depression.

4.   Allergies: If you have seasonal allergies, you may find that your mood is influenced by the time of year you tend to have symptoms. Constant sneezing, watery eyes, and itchiness can also lead to fatigue, especially if they interfere with sleep.

5.   Sleep: A person's mood can also be heavily influenced by the amount and quality of sleep they get. A person who is sleep-deprived (especially when chronic) may experience intense mood fluctuations as well as other psychiatric

symptoms. Maybe your colleague just isn't much of a morning person, but their mood naturally lifts as they wake up and they feel more prepared for the day ahead. The body's circadian rhythm, which is known for influencing when we sleep, also drives our mood throughout the day to a certain extent.

6.   Medications: Starting or stopping a prescription medication can also affect a person's mood. While medications such as antidepressants and mood stabilizers are expected to affect a person's moods, medications prescribed for other reasons may also cause mood swings as a side effect. Even though mood changes can be a symptom of depression or another mental health condition, some medications used to treat these disorders can also cause changes in mood. Sometimes, these mood shifts indicate that the medication isn't the right choice for treatment, or that the diagnosis someone has been given may not be correct.

7.   Substance Use: People who are dealing with substance use disorders may also be more prone to experiencing extreme shifts in mood, especially when they are unable to get or use a substance, or when they are trying to quit a drug and experiencing withdrawal. When misused, medications known to cause mood changes can have especially severe effects. For example, symptoms may be erratic and even life-threatening if a person (such as an athlete) misuses steroid medications.

8.	Hormones: Other possible causes of mood swings may stem from an imbalance of the brain chemicals that are associated with mood regulation, as in the case of bipolar disorder. Fluctuations in brain chemicals can also be a normal function, such as the hormonal changes of the menstrual cycle. For the same reason, mood swings are also common in response to other causes of shifting levels of hormones (especially estrogen), such as pregnancy and menopause. However, a person's risk for depression is increased during these times as well, so mood swings can also be a sign of a mental health condition.

Back to our discussion above, Mood swings are common behavioral currency in people with lower Emotional Quotient, but this is at least predictable. You can adapt to this by carefully tuning in to their emotions and remembering that they are likely to react in an exaggerated manner to both good and bad events. The more someone's mood fluctuates, and the more they overreact to circumstances and situations, the bigger your need to sync to their emotions and ride their mood waves—so you don't end up crushed by them.

•	MAKE THINGS EXPLICIT

People differ in their ability to make sense of ambivalent or ambiguous real-world situations, and most of the people problems we encounter at work fit into this bucket. Regardless of your own Emotional Quotient, if you work for someone who is not naturally adept at interpreting your own emotions and intentions, it is key that you help them understand you. Use explicit communication, put things in writing, set out clearly what you think and want, and ensure that your message is understood, without assuming that any subtleties may be captured.

- BE A SOURCE OF INSIGHTS

You will gain a lot of brownie points with your boss if you can leverage your intuition—assuming your Emotional Quotient is higher than theirs'—and help them interpret other people's intentions, feelings, and thoughts. In other words, you become an emotional and social "consigliere" to your boss by effectively boosting their ability to make sense of and influence others. This means making them a little bit more streetwise and improving their basic people skills.

- AVOID BEING A STRESS AGENT

Even if you cannot put into practice the arguably challenging suggestions outlined in the first three points, you should at least avoid being a source of stress for your boss. This means staying calm, reducing the likelihood of conflict, and acting like a soothing and calming influence for them, which essentially is the exact opposite of their behavior. Note that managers–like people in general–have a tendency to prefer working with people who are like them, but this is not the case when they have a lower Emotional Quotient. The more volatile and excitable you are, the more you will enjoy the company of stable and predictable people, even if it means that your employees are doubling as informal therapists or coaches.

Finally, remember that while Emotional Quotient is generally advantageous at work—you are better off having more of it—quite a few of the most sought-after skillsets actually benefit from lower Emotional Quotient. For instance, people tasked with creative or artistic jobs, those who need to be skeptical of others (chief legal officer), or be always paranoid about unlikely threats (air traffic controllers), show lower than average Emotional Quotient levels even among successful performers. Many jobs that require minimal interpersonal contact with others (remote IT or academic jobs) are far less dependent on people skills and Emotional Quotient.

We must learn to embrace individual differences, not just tolerate them. An organizational culture made purely of high Emotional Quotient individuals would probably be closer to a happy cult than an innovative and exciting venture.

HABITS OF PEOPLE WITH REMARKABLE MENTAL TOUGHNESS

First, the definition: "The ability to work hard and respond resiliently to failure and adversity; the inner quality that enables individuals to work hard and stick to their long-term passions and goals."

Now the word: Grit.

The definition of grit almost perfectly describes qualities every successful person possesses, because mental toughness builds the foundations for long-term success.

For example, successful people are great at delaying gratification. Successful people are great at withstanding temptation. Successful people are great at overcoming fear in order to do what they need to do. (Of course, that doesn't mean they aren't scared--that does mean they're brave. Big difference.) Successful people don't just prioritize. They consistently keep doing what they have decided is most important.

All those qualities require mental strength and toughness--so it's no coincidence those are some of the qualities of remarkably successful people.

Here are ways you can become mentally stronger--and as a result more successful:

1.   Always act as if you are in total control.

There's a quote that says "Survivors are not always the strongest; sometimes they are the smartest, but more often simply the luckiest".

The meaning of being strong in this quote refers to being strong physically. Being smart has to deal with how mentally strong you are. Just because your physicality does not work for you does not mean you are lucky. Your mental intelligence determines how strong you are and how well you can survive against all odds; not by strength or power.

Many people feel luck has a lot to do with success or failure. If they succeed, luck favored them, and if they fail, luck was against them.

Most successful people do feel good luck played some role in their success. But they don't wait for good luck or worry about bad luck. They act as if success or failure is totally within their control. If they succeed, they caused it. If they fail, they caused it.

By not wasting mental energy worrying about what might happen to you, you can put all your effort into making things happen. And then, if you get lucky, hey, you're even better off. You can't control luck, but you can definitely control yourself.

2.   Put aside things you have no ability to impact.

Mental strength is like muscle strength--no one has an unlimited supply. So why waste your power on things you can't control?

For some people, it's politics. For others, it's family. For others, it's global warming. Whatever it is, you care, and you want others to care.

Fine. Do what you can do: Vote. Lend a listening ear. Recycle, and reduce your carbon footprint. Do what you can do. Be your own change--but don't try to make everyone else change because they won't. Every change occurs as a result of the inner decisions we make, so don't try to make or force anybody to change. Everything is within.

3.   See the past as valuable training and nothing more.

The past is valuable. Learn from your mistakes. Learn from the mistakes of others. Then let it go.

Easier said than done? It depends on your perspective. When something bad happens to you, see it as an opportunity to learn something you didn't know. Consider your mistakes as part of your future success. When another person makes a mistake, don't just learn from it--see it as an opportunity to be kind, forgiving, and understanding.

The past is just training; it doesn't define you. Think about what went wrong but only in terms of how you will make sure that next time, you and the people around you will know how to make sure it goes right.

4.	Celebrate the success of others.

Many people--I guarantee you know at least a few--see success as a zero-sum game: There's only so much to go around. When someone else shines, they think that diminishes the light from their stars.

Resentment sucks up a massive amount of mental energy, the energy that is better applied elsewhere.

When a friend does something awesome, that doesn't preclude you from doing something awesome. In fact, where success is concerned, birds of a feather tend to flock together--so draw your successful friends even closer.

Here in Nigeria, Africa, your friends start to envy you once to attain an excellent result. This is one of the reasons we can't develop as a nation. I have had so many of such and I am still experiencing it up till now. It hurts me to see my friends leave me but on the other hand, I would be severely harmed if I don't let them go. So I don't force anybody to be my friend. If you want to stay, you can stay and if you want to leave, you are free to leave any time that is convenient for you.

Don't resent awesomeness. Create and celebrate awesomeness, wherever you find it, and in time you'll find even more of it in yourself.

5.   Never allow yourself to whine. (Or complain. Or criticize.)

Your words have power, especially over you. Whining about your problems always makes you feel worse, not better. So if something is wrong, don't waste time complaining. Put that mental energy into making the situation better. Unless you want to whine about it forever, eventually you'll have to make it better.

So why waste time? Fix it now. Don't talk about what's wrong. Talk about how you'll make things better, even if that conversation is only with yourself. And do the same with your friends or colleagues. Don't just serve as a shoulder they can cry on. Friends don't let friends whine; friends help friends make their lives better.

6.   Focus only on impressing yourself.

Let me remind you that human beings are equal in rank. It is the qualities of the person which earn respect rather than the quality and quantity of his possessions.

No one likes you for your clothes, your car, your possessions, your title, or your accomplishments. Those are all things. People may like your things--but that doesn't mean they like you.

Sure, superficially they might seem to like you, but what's superficial is also insubstantial, and a relationship not based on substance is not a real relationship.

Genuine relationships make you happier, and you'll only form genuine relationships when you stop trying to impress and start trying to just be yourself.

And you'll have a lot more mental energy to spend on the people who really do matter in your life.

7.   Count your blessings.

Take a second every night before you turn out the light and, at that moment, quit worrying about what you don't have. Quit worrying about what others have that you don't. Think about what you do have. You have a lot to be thankful for. Even the Bible says, in all situations, always give thanks to the Lord. Feels pretty good, doesn't it?

Feeling better about yourself is the best way of all to recharge your mental batteries. Sometimes I do think I'm the most complete man in the world. One in particular which I use to think about is me being the right for every girl and one day, my girlfriend told me "Jade, you are the kind of man every girl will always want to date". That gave me a very deep additional impression about myself.

OVERTHINKING AND MENTAL TOUGHNESS

More often it has been reported that mental toughness results in overthinking which is harmful to human health. How to stop overthinking is an essential aspect of personal success and personal growth.

In order to progress in our human development, we must take time to contemplate personal development as well as various topics of personal growth, such as how to stop overthinking, which is exactly the intention of these virtual personal coaching sessions.

Personal success is achieved through the disciplined execution of a fully established personal development plan.

These virtual personal coaching sessions are to assist you in your self-improvement, personal growth, and personal development.

Overthinking is a natural part of life for many of us, even when we're not aware we're doing it. Research has shown that overthinking is prevalent in young and middle-aged adults, with 73% of 25-35 year-olds identified as overthinkers.

More women (57%) find themselves overthinking than men (43%), which is a significant difference. This means the majority of women are overthinkers, and the majority of overthinkers are women.

Take your time with this topic, carefully consider your responses to the questions and write them down. Personal growth is not supposed to be easy, it takes courage to face yourself. But when you develop the courage and mental strength to do actually this, you will be building confidence.

Questions to Uncover Beliefs about Overthinking:

• Do you believe clarity and depth of thoughts are created when you are overthinking?

• Do you believe the brain has a limited capacity for thought?

• What do you believe are the most effective tools for how to stop overtaking?

Unsupportive Beliefs about Overthinking:

• I don't have time to escape my overthinking.

• You can stop overthinking if you're mentally strong enough.

• Overthinking has no adverse effects on decision making.

Mental Strength Beliefs about Overthinking:

• Mental and cognitive rest and recovery are as important as physical rest and recovery.

• Psychological rest is a catalyst for creativity.

• Escaping from overthinking will boost your physical and mental energy

Outrageous Questions about Overthinking:

• Are you using the space between your thoughts for rest and recovery as a peak performance stagey?

• If you built in more mental rest and recovery into your daily schedule would you be more successful?

• What mental recovery strategies have you used in the past and how did they work for you?

Reflective Questions about Overthinking:

•   Do you believe mental recovery is an excuse for goofing off, or it is an effective peak performance strategy?

•   Is it possible you are underestimating the magnitude of the impact escaping overthinking can have on your reasoning ability?

•   How do you make the distinction between emotional, mental, physical, and spiritual overload?

Mental Strength Coaching on Overthinking:

Overthinking isn't something you're born doing, it's a learned habit you form over time, probably as a defense mechanism to the possibility of failure. So before going any further, let's see what we can do about it.

One reason that we may be primed to ruminate: Our memories are linked by powerful emotional associations. When an unpleasant event puts us in a despondent mood, it's easier to recall other times when we've felt terrible.

If you find yourself overthinking, you need to change the channel in your mind immediately. Simple, right? It mostly is. The caveat here is that while the solution is simple, putting it into action takes ongoing practice.

How to Stop Overthinking Everything: 12 Simple Habits

What is holding people back from the life that they truly want to live? I would say that one very common and destructive thing is that they don't know how to stop overthinking.

They overthink every little problem until it becomes bigger and scarier than it actually is. They overthink positive things until they don't look so positive anymore (and as the anxiety starts to build).

Or overanalyze and deconstruct things and so the happiness that comes from just enjoying something at the moment disappears.

Now, thinking things through can be a great thing of course. But getting lost in a sort of overthinking disorder can result in becoming someone who stands still in life. In becoming someone who self-sabotages the good things that happen in life.

I used to overthink things a lot and it held me back in ways that weren't fun at all. But in the past five years or so I've learned how to make this issue so small that it very rarely pops up anymore. And if it does then I know what to do to overcome it.

I will like to share twelve habits that have helped me in a big way to become a simpler and smarter thinker and to live a happier and less fearful life.

1.   Put things into a wider perspective.

It's very easy to fall into the trap of overthinking minor things in life. So when you are thinking and thinking about something ask yourself:

Will this matter in 5 years? Or even in 5 weeks?

I've found that widening the perspective by using this simple question can quickly snap me out of overthinking and help me to let go of that situation.

It allows me to finally stop thinking about something and to focus my time and energy on something else that actually does matter to me.

2.   Set short time-limits for decisions.

If you do not have a time-limit for when you must make a decision and take action then you can just keep turning your thoughts around and around and view them from all angles in your mind for a very long time.

So learn to become better at making decisions and to spring into action by setting deadlines in your daily life. No matter if it's a small or bigger decision.

Here's what has worked for me:

• For small decisions like if should go and do the dishes, respond to an email or work out I usually give myself 30 seconds or less to make a decision.

• For somewhat larger decisions that would have taken me days or weeks to think through in the past I use a deadline for 30 minutes or for the end of the workday.

3. Stop setting your day up for stress and overthinking.

You can't totally avoid overwhelming or very stressful days. But you can minimize the number of them in your month and year by getting a good start to your day and by not setting yourself up for unnecessary stress, overthinking, and suffering.

Three things that help me with that are:

• Get a good start.

I've mentioned this earlier before now and with good reason. Because how you start your day tends to often set the tone for your day.

A stressed morning leads to a stressed day. Consuming negative information as you ride the bus to your job tends to lead to more pessimistic thoughts during the rest of your day.

While for example reading something uplifting over breakfast, getting some exercise, and then get started with your most important task right now sets a good tone for the day and will help you to stay positive.

- Single-task and take regular breaks.

When I am in class, I play a lot. So it hardly appears like I am a serious type. My course mates do tell me that I am not serious but the fact that I play a lot does not mean that I am not serious.

This will help you to keep a sharp focus during your day and to get what's most important done, while also allowing you to rest and recharge so you don't start to run on fumes.

And this somewhat relaxed mindset but with the narrow focus will help you to think clearly and decisively and avoid winding up in a stressed and overthinking headspace.

- Minimize your daily input.

Too much information, too many times of just taking a few minutes to check your inbox, Facebook or Twitter account, or how your blog or website is doing leads to more input and clutter in your mind as your day progresses.

And so it becomes harder to think in a simple and clear way and easier to lapse back into that familiar overthinking habit.

4.   Become a person of action.

When you know how to get started with taking action consistently each day then you'll procrastinate less by overthinking.

Setting deadlines and a good tone for the day are two things that have helped me to become much more of a person of action.

Taking small steps forward and only focusing on getting one small step done at a time is another habit that has worked really well.

It works so well because you do not feel overwhelmed and so you do not want to flee into procrastination or lazy inaction.

And even though you may be afraid, taking just a step is such a small thing that you do not get paralyzed in fear.

5.   Realize that you cannot control everything.

Trying to think things through 50 times can be a way to try to control everything. To cover every eventuality so you don't risk making a mistake, fail or looking like a fool.

But those things are a part of living a life where you truly stretch your comfort zone. Everyone whom you may admire and have lived a life that inspires you has failed. They have made mistakes.

But in most cases, they've also seen these things as valuable feedback to learn from.

Those things that may look negative have taught them a lot and have been invaluable to help them to grow.

So stop trying to control everything. Trying to do so simply doesn't work because no one can see all possible scenarios in advance.

This is of course easier said than done. So do it in small steps if you like.

6.   Say stop in a situation where you know you cannot think straight.

Sometimes when I'm hungry or when I'm lying in bed and are about to go to sleep negative thoughts start buzzing around in my mind.

In the past, they could do quite a bit of damage. Nowadays I've become good at catching them quickly and saying to myself:

No, no, we are not going to think about this now.

I know that when I'm hungry or sleepy then my mind sometimes tends to be vulnerable to not thinking clearly and to negativity.

I don't swallow my words so I follow up my "no, no…" phrase and I say to myself that I will think this situation or issue through when I know that my mind will work much better. For example, after I've eaten something or in the morning after I have gotten my hours of sleep.

It took a bit of practice to get this to work but I've gotten pretty good at postponing thinking in this way. And I know from experience that when I revisit a situation with some level-headed thinking then in 80% of the cases the issue is very small to nonexistent.

And if there is a real issue then my mind is prepared to deal with it in a much better and more constructive way.

7.   Don't get lost in vague fears.

Another trap I've fallen into many times that have spurred on overthinking is that I've gotten lost in vague fears about a situation in my life.

And so my mind running wild has created disaster scenarios about what could happen if I do something.

So I've learned to ask myself: honestly, what is the worst that could happen?

And when I've figured out what the worst that could happen actually is then I can also spend a little time to think about what I can do if that often pretty unlikely thing happens.

I've found that the worst that could realistically happen is usually something that is not as scary as what my mind running wild with vague fear could produce.

Finding clarity in this way usually only takes a few minutes and a bit of energy and it can save you a lot of time and suffering.

8.   Work out.

This might sound a bit odd. But working out can really help with letting go of inner tensions and worries.

It most often makes me feel more decisive and when I was more of an overthinker, then it was often my go-to method of changing the headspace I was into a more constructive one.

9.   Get plenty of good quality sleep.

I think this is one of the most commonly neglected factors when it comes to keeping a positive mindset and not get lost in negative thought habits.

Because when you haven't slept enough then you become more vulnerable.

Vulnerable to worrying and pessimism. To not thinking as clearly as you usually do. And to get lost in thoughts going around and around in your mind as you overthink.

So let me share a couple of my favorite tips that help me to sleep better:

- Keep it cool.

It can feel nice at first to get into a warm bedroom. But I've found that I sleep better and more calmly with fewer scary or negative dreams if I keep the bedroom cool.

- Keep the earplugs nearby.

If you, like me, are easily awoken by noises then a pair of simple earplugs can be a life-saver. These inexpensive items have helped me to get a good night's sleep and sleep through snorers, noisy cats, and other disturbances more times than I can remember.

- Don't try to force yourself to go to sleep.

If you don't feel sleepy then don't get into bed and try to force yourself to go to sleep. That, at least in my experience, only leads to tossing and turning in my bed for an hour or more.

A better solution in these situations is to wind down for an extra 20-30 minutes on the couch with, for example, some reading. This helps me to go to sleep faster and, in the end, get more sleep.

10.   Spend more of your time in the present moment.

By being in the present moment in your everyday life rather than in the past or a possible future in your mind you can replace more and more of the time you usually spend on overthinking things with just being here right now instead.

Three ways that I often use to reconnect with the present moment are:

•   Slow down and catch your breath

Slow down how you do whatever you are doing right now. Move slower, talk slower or ride your bicycle more slowly for example. By doing so you become more aware of how you use your body and what is happening all around you right now.

•   Tell yourself: Now I am…

I often tell myself this: Now I am here. And here could be brushing my teeth. Taking a walk in the woods. Or doing the dishes.

This simple reminder helps my mind to stop wandering and brings my focus back to what is happening at this moment.

- Disrupt and reconnect.

If you feel you are getting lost in overthinking, then disrupt that thought by – in your mind – shouting this to yourself: STOP!

Then reconnect with the present moment by taking just 1-2 minutes to focus fully on what is going on around you. Take it all in with all your senses. Feel it, hear it, smell it, see it and sense it on your skin.

11.   Spend more of your time with people who do not overthink things.

Your social environment plays a big part. And not just the people and groups close to you in real life. But also what you read, listen to and watch. The blogs, books, forums, movies, podcasts, and music in your life.

So, think about if there are any sources in your life – close by or further away – that encourages and tends to create more overthinking in your mind. And think about what people or sources that has the opposite effect on you.

Find ways to spend more of your time and attention with the people and input that have a positive effect on your thinking and less on the influences that tend to strengthen your overthinking habit.

12.   Be aware of the issue (and remind yourself throughout your day)

Being aware of your challenge is important to break the habit of overthinking. But if you're thinking that you'll just remember to stop overthinking during your normal day then you're likely just fooling yourself.

At least if you're anything like me. Because I needed help. It wasn't hard to get it though. I just created a few reminders.

My main one was a note on the whiteboard I had on one of my walls at the time. It said, "Keep things extremely simple". Seeing this many times during my day helped me to snap out of overthinking faster and to overtime greatly minimize this negative habit.

Two other kinds of reminders that you can use are:

•   A small written note.

Simply use a post-it note or something similar and write down my whiteboard phrase, a question like "Am I overcomplicating this?" or some other reminder that appeals to you.

Put that note where you cannot avoid seeing it like for example on your bedside table, your bathroom mirror, or beside your computer screen.

- A reminder on your smartphone.

Write down one of the phrases above or one of your own choosing in a reminder app on your smartphone. I for example use my Android phone.

HOW TO BE A HIGHLY SENSITIVE PERSON (HSP)

Responsiveness, high sensitivity, and tactile response to processing are words used in this book to identify a single inherent personality characteristic described as an understanding of the subtleties in stimuli as well as a capacity to be distracted by too many stimuli. This improved vision is not a function of the sense organs, but rather a brain that demonstrates especially profoundly a technique for processing information.

Sensitivity is observed in about 15 to 20 percent of the population. Interestingly, in most mammals, it has also been observed in almost the same percentage, from fruit flies to primates, although the molecular type and appearance differ with the species, of course. Its distribution is rather bimodal than usual; that is, people tend to have the feature or not. Midway there aren't many.

Biologists often apply two general animal techniques, which give rise to two forms of inherent personality with different names, such as brazen versus cautious, hawk versus dove, or unresponsive versus responsive. The former appears to be the bulk. Their technique is to move swiftly and aggressively into feeding and mating opportunities if possible without much preliminary examination of the situation. By deliberately studying the subtleties in a scenario before behaving, the reactive minority developed a protective strategy by minimizing risks compared with the more impulsive or confident 80 percent. Both approaches-" thinking first "and "acting promptly" be effective, depending on environmental conditions.

For individuals, for functional magnetic resonance imaging and more commonly in thinking and feeling before and during the action, the more sensitive technique of checking the world and listening to stimulus information was found. Such a technique makes a greater awareness of the subtleties and consequences. This in turn leads to increased levels of consciousness and imagination, for example. On the negative side, this intricate processing creates a greater potential to get over-stimulated and disturbed by stressful events in life.

As far as gender is involved, there are as many receptive people born to both gender sides, and while the existence of testosterone may have some later impact, they often perceive sensitivity differently depending on the society they reside in. If some men are sensitive and their culture disapproves of such, these men generally tend to cover up their vulnerability to look more like a typical male. For example, there was originally a question about crying easily on the scale, to which many respondents agreed, but the men did so much less. In reality, sensitive men were still slightly less likely to claim they cry easily than other men. Eliminating elements like this however did not change the overall gender result, which was that men scored lower. That is probably because of their overall scale impression. Sensitive men definitely have different problems than sensitive women and are likely to face bigger problems overall.

The bottom line is that Sensitivity is an innate characteristic found in 20 percent of humans, and also in most animals. It seems to benefit from a technique of deliberately analyzing knowledge before behaving, which contributes to the comprehension of subtleties but also to potentially over-stimulation. There are as many reactive men as women, but men are more likely to conceal this tendency and typically have more trouble.

The HSP appears to be particularly sensitive to pain, caffeine consequences, and violent movies. Highly sensitive individuals in their life are also made extremely anxious by bright lights, strong smells, and shifts. You will discover hundreds of new coping strategies in this companion book to The Highly Sensitive Individual to keep calm and quiet in today's over-stimulating environment, turning your anxiety into inner peace and joy.

HSPs will consider growing up daunting in a culture that promotes violence and over-stimulation. John grew up in the era of legends like John Wayne when real men should be big, rugged and quiet. He didn't fit in at school as a highly sensitive kid and thought there was something inherently wrong with him. He surmised at an early age that he was a bad person because he thought the deception was shameful being emotional. Virtually all the mental distress he experienced growing up was directly related to a lack of understanding of his very reactive nervous system.

As an adult, you may still suffer from an incomprehension about your vulnerability. Our fast-paced and violent modern industrialized environment is having an adverse effect on HSPs. You will quickly get tired, forever.

Sensitivity as a clinical service

High sensitivity to inherent personality is a normal variation. It has a high prevalence and has many benefits. It is not a category diagnosis. While the mental disorder is orthogonal. Any sensitive person has diagnosable conditions as do some non-sensitive people. Most don't like what insensitive people do.

However, the extremely sensitive were shown to be more vulnerable to stress, anxiety, and shyness if they had rough childhoods, but with sufficient evidence of childhood is no more predictive of this characteristic than nonsensitive persons. Indeed, sensitive children seem to profit from good childhood more than others. Yet many have impairments of varying degrees, especially mood and anxiety disorders.

On the other side, one will see highly sensitive patients who do not have a condition but who have been diagnosed with one, and some will have a disease but are misdiagnosed. (You may also see a lot of people who believe they're highly sensitive, hear about it, and actually don't have a disease, rather). Sometimes, the trait described here is said to be at the high end of this spectrum. Nevertheless, the requirements for autism or Asperger's syndrome do not correlate with high sensitivity as described here and observed in 20 percent of the population. Many autistic people are disturbed by high levels of specific types of stimuli, but other kinds, particularly social signals, will unfazed them. Conversely, sensitive individuals can handle high levels of stimulus without becoming utterly confused or aggressive, and they are using more acceptable ways to reduce stimuli as they develop.

Furthermore, the discomfort of autism is attributed to the inappropriate use of sensory information, which is not transmitted to deeper levels. Sensitive people do not persevere as autistic people do, although they show high levels of empathy as well as satisfactory to excellent social skills, especially in familiar settings. Problems of sensory integration are also associated with adaptation to the application. But the impairment or disease of sensory integration relates to particular soft neurological problems that typically react well to medication. Through these therapies, certain sensitive individuals (and indeed most sedentary people despite their temperament) can change. We will not however delete the features mentioned below.

The disability is something that you expect will improve or decrease. While sensitive people's lives will change with an understanding of their characteristics and they can learn ways to adapt, no therapy can eradicate inherent high sensitivity, and there is no justification to want to do so despite its benefits in certain contexts.

Gender and ethnicity differences

A simpler way of thinking about this characteristic is that it is a common variation in the person, much like gender, but only in a minority of the population, much like a particular ethnicity. Since many people respond yes to each item on the HSP Scale, while many others respond no to each item, it could be argued that this difference is at least as powerful in its effect as gender and ethnicity. It is, however, a largely invisible gap, and these create unique social challenges for those who have them.

There are specific problems correlated with being highly sensitive, as with gender and ethnicity, some of them related to the condition itself, such as being quickly over-aroused, and some due to the culture in which it is located. Elementary school children with the characteristic, for example, are common with peers in China; they aren't in Canada. Thus sensitive individuals may have high or low self-esteem, depending on the culture.

There are also conditions that have nothing to do with susceptibility itself but the character brings a certain color to the condition. For example, as they understand the role of over-stimulation in their symptoms, a certain percentage of sensitive people with panic disorder recover with relative ease, while panic attacks in non-sensitive people are less likely to be treated in this manner.

HSP compared to another personality trait

The HSP Scale overlaps with but is not equivalent to introversion tests, since about 30 percent of sensitive individuals are considered to be extroverts. This statistic relies on the test of introversion used, as these tests do not correspond well in and of themselves.

The association is generally higher about neuroticism. One explanation is that, once again, highly sensitive individuals with a difficult childhood are more likely to be depressed, nervous, and shy— that is, have more negative effects (the common concept of neuroticism as a characteristic of personality) than nonsensitive people with the same degree of childhood struggle and trauma. Many sensitive individuals will have had rough childhoods in any random sample, so they increase the mean neuroticism ratings for the whole vulnerable group unless the context for the childhood is statistically regulated.

Shyness follows the same trend but is only apparent if a negative effect is also present. That is, if sensitive people had challenging childhoods and this has culminated in high levels of negative effect, they are more likely to be cautious. Not the bad childhood of every sensitive person contributes to negative effects. The results of unfortunate experiences are shyness and negative effect, not the trait itself.

The bottom line is that Introversion, neuroticism, or shyness is not the same as high sensitivity.

The deep thinking typical to all highly sensitive individuals contributes to the following characteristics. This list is based on private published data and some other evidence, or in some instances, some extensive experience, scientifically and in study interviews, except where noted. No sensitive person would have all of them but should have a wide variety of them, as opposed to having a handful (only sitting on the margins or merely becoming conscientious), which could be attributable to something other than a profound genetic difference.

• After approaching it for a while, and usually investigating a condition more by watching and contemplating rather than going inside.

• Being very conscious of the subtleties or the minor changes.

• Wanting to analyze any aspect and possible outcome before deciding–"do it once and do it correctly"–as compared to the propensity of the majority to determine sooner. For example, this results in being quicker than nonsensitive people when it comes to making decisions, being more mindful of risks and benefits, and being seen as sluggish but accurate.

• Being more mindful of other people's thoughts and reactions, gathering more knowledge from nonverbal signals, and accurately predicting attributable to intuiting the likely effects of a scenario on others.

• Having suffered more damage from poor experiences in childhood or adulthood, but likely benefiting more from extraordinarily positive settings (skilled parenting or childhood instruction, or conscientious adult management).

• Acting more conscientiously because they are heavily attuned to causes and consequences— how things turned out as they are and how they turn out, depending on what's done. More often they think, "What if everyone has left their trash behind?" "If I don't complete my work on time, I'll slow down everyone."

• Expressing uncommon consideration about social justice and the atmosphere and an extraordinary degree of sensitivity, even in infancy.

• Being quickly over-stimulated. The more stimulation for anyone, the more arousal and overarousal it leads to poorer performance. Yet sensitive people become overcome by fewer stimuli earlier, and thus experience more problems or setbacks in extremely stressful circumstances (e.g. competitions, recitals, public speaking, encountering trusted visitors, being taught or under supervision, scheduled training, and also areas that are loud, busy, etc.).

• Feeling creative, talented, or enthusiastic about the arts.

• Strongly interested in spirituality and often involved in a particular practice;

• Expressing a greater emotional response to events that elicit close, but less so, emotions in others;

• Note extreme pain due to modifications.

• If asked to report unusually vivid dreams can entirely narrate deeply what had happened.

• Remembering any of these features first appearing in puberty. Complaining about too distracting or unesthetic conditions. Sensitive teens seem to handle loud music, crowds, and multitasking more, but that improves in the late 20s.

• Getting physical resilience — faster startling response; more aggressive immune system (e.g., more touch allergies; Bell, 1992)—and stronger responsiveness to discomfort, stimulants (e.g., caffeine), and most medicines.

• To talk in a considerate, often indirect, way.

• To consider that nature is exceptionally soothing, relaxing, or more affected by its majesty. Fond of plants, animals, and being close to or in water.

Impact of their great emotional nature

One explanation why sensitive people are so interesting and challenging to deal with, and so vulnerable to misdiagnosis, is that all sensitive individuals respond to a specific emotion-generating circumstance more intensely, albeit in a normal way. It's an argument not reflected explicitly on the questionnaire, partially in order to avoid gender bias.

If a desire for better processing of information is the underlying reason that explains the highly sensitive's different behaviors, how does this lead to stronger emotional reactions? One could assume this reflection to have a calming effect, but sensory exposure to perception necessarily involves greater emotionality, for at least two purposes. Next, emotion controls cognitive processing, since nothing is processed long without an important or interesting emotional assessment. Secondly, production influences emotion, in that the more something that has emotional significance becomes stored, the more emotion it produces.

The greater emotionality is linked to the experience I have already mentioned, where sensitive people with troubled childhood are more susceptible to depression, anxiety, and shyness than those with the same degree of distress. The highly sensitive, though, are also more responsive to strong positive responses than others, such as reacting to incentives.

To characterize this characteristic as an inherent "extreme susceptibility" or "proneness to negative effect," or "neuroticism" in that context, would be as limited a description as using "pronounced skin cancer" as the only word to be skinned equally.

Nevertheless, it remains the case that highly sensitive individuals experience stronger emotional responses, a substantial consideration to keep in mind for psychotherapists. A mild criticism can evoke shame. Mild appreciation will give rise to euphoria or perhaps a misconception of your emotions.

What you don't notice about the highly sensitive people

It's also helpful to think about how individuals who are not highly sensitive view themselves. Since these are most people, much can be ascertained clearly by knowing what most people enjoy or don't bother. You are not typically disturbed by noise, visual disturbance, sudden change, or other facets of a susceptible person's atmosphere or perception that would over-stimulate. This is very clearly illustrated by the acceptable level of arousal in work environments and by the pleasurable degree of it in leisure activities and the media. The ridiculous majority mainly love the rapidly shifting visual stimulation of video games, TV ads, and action movies. During the holidays they prefer street fairs, major sports activities, and shopping malls. Some love horror films, dangerous sports, and watching dramas that contain disturbing crime. Nor do they care too much about the potential until they are found out or become costly about the effects of some practice.

A large number of people, for example, refuse to get screened for prostate, lung, and breast cancer.

Once again, the rest take risks with less thorough planning, choosing solely from what is common behavior. ("I never expected that to happen.") Highly sensitive people take chances, but they do take care. Of starters, they appear to be health specialists in a dangerous sport and are much less likely to get injured. When they lose at something, instead of dwelling on their mistake and adjusting tactics as the minority does, they want to attempt again instantly. The attitude in the majority loves both forms of gambling. We are less influenced by real or perceived failure or other financial or error. They are usually less emotionally reactive. And they can display more of their feelings, such as expressing anger over the service they provide, even though public anger communication is typically socially dangerous and highly stimulating. It is also common for most people to speak in a direct manner most of the time, with less care about how their sound or word choice may influence the audience as they consider others to be fairly imperturbable like themselves.

Some people love nature, and there, some find shelter. But the nonsensitive prefer to see it more as a way to perform things and are less worried about animals suffering rather than their own livestock. We can follow a faith, but less doubt it. Relatively less are thinking with spiritual matters, religion, or "the meaning of life." But let's go back to creating a buzz among highly sensitive individuals by portraying one as he or she would be in your workplace.

It can be useful to note how reactive people do not match the other patients in that the latter are not readily over-stimulated — affected by noise or sudden change, for example— and are less likely to notice subtleties such as shifts in your workplace. Although the following is over-generalizing, nonsensitive patients will be the maker of video games, fans, team sports, and action movies; not disturbed by violence; take more risks and love doing so; plan less for activities; and talk more clearly, with no clues. They are reluctant to use nature more than as a place of solace for leisure, and though moral, they have offered their convictions fewer.

HIGH SENSITIVY AND HIGH SENSATION SEEKING

Highly sensitive people may also be seekers of high stimuli. It is somewhat counterintuitive but you need to address this early enough to understand this significant feature variability. Those two features are independent of each other, regulated by different brain pathways. To date, it is believed that the desire for pleasure is triggered by regions of excessively intense reward, which are more closely associated with dopamine. Sensitivity is less well known but is possibly caused in part by enhanced activity in areas that facilitate action inhibition along with warning focus, a trend associated with low serotonin, providing ideal conditions for deeper processing of information. Hence, the correct understanding of high sensitivity is not an evasion of stimuli, even if it contributes to overstimulation avoidance.

In reality, they respond more to performance and to reward than others. Rather, a need to analyze a circumstance before behaving is the underlying incentive provided by the condition, so the opposite of being extremely sensitive is being impulsive.

Sensational-seeking sensitive people are boredom-prone. Like Susan has said, without any other ventures of her existence, she would not be a successful stay-at-home mom. Generally, they'll enjoy trying new restaurants and new cuisines, not the same old haunt (unless they feel over-stimulated). Susan loved trying out new work. We don't like watching the same film twice unless it's a really nice one.

They hang gliding or traveling to exotic places but they are never impulsive and plan the operation in advance, doing everything they can to ensure their safety. They may like a surprise, but they don't like surprises or high risks. But since the dopamine-driven reward system creates a high desire to engage or act immediately, while the avoidance system's aim is to do just that, being high on both factors can be difficult to create a delay for checking things out. "It's like living with one foot on the floor, one foot on the brakes," as one person with this mix called it. The highly sensitive person can also be a strong feeling hunter. We are independent features. Sensitivity is the inverse of impulsiveness, not simply a fear of novelty.

Societal values and sensitivity

There have been more tolerance of empathy and some wondrous changes in societal values in the last ten to twenty years. While most people have been brought up to act stern and hide feelings, many modern men now believe that empathy is a positive feature. In recent years, several reports about the connection between stress-related diseases and intense work conditions have been published in the media, offering people the opportunity to doubt whether operating under severe pressure is worth damaging to their wellbeing.

Although there is now a subculture of enlightened people who accept awareness as a valued characteristic for both men and women, there has been a disturbing increase in overstimulation in our community. The sweet I Want to Hold Your Hand was a popular song in the '60s, although today the recognized raucous music is often packed with words of cursing and abuse. Cutting classrooms was one of the worst crimes in school a generation ago, while at several urban schools now there are security guards and metal detectors to deter school shootings.

Three or four television stations remained in the 1950s, although today we are inundated with close to 1000 stations streaming a plethora of shows riddled with graphic sex and gratuitous violence. The home telephone was substituted by millions of cell phones that are commonplace to modern society, generating a worldwide cacophony of clamor. Recently I was trekking up a majestic mountain peak in Colorado, loving the quiet and beautiful natural setting when a man charged past me yelled into his cell phone, "I told you to get the stock sold!" Thirty or forty years ago most people shopped in small neighborhood shops and had a personal relationship with the store owner or clerk.

Virtually all mom-and-pop shops have been substituted in most urban environments by massive, impersonal companies that could be named "Stimulation Depot" or "Noise R Us." You have to compete with hundreds of other customers as you desperately seek shopping among thousands of items, or walk around trying to find assistance from the few frustrated and underpaid clerks. You may understand why HSPs still consider shopping an emotionally exhausting process nowadays, because of this intense level of stimulus. There was a video showing a young woman doing toothpaste shopping. As she decided to choose from a plethora of toothpaste products, she was overwhelmed: anticavity, fluoride, no fluoride, antigingivitis, extra whitener, spray, lined, anti-stain for cigarettes, gum safety, 15 percent big savings, 20 percent on extra-large. She felt so exhausted after evaluating the plethora of items she selected, that she went home to lie down from fatigue.

Age is a determining factor in our response to stimuli. Overstimulation affects children and older people more deeply. Since kids have not yet developed the ability to articulate themselves, they still respond intensively.

When adolescents and young adults, HSPs are more sensitive to overstimulation. Many teens with HSP will typically also handle listening to loud music and drinking all-night hours. When you mature, the arousal potential declines, and it's normal for many middle-aged HSPs to go to bed early and avoid a lot of going out. You always have to find a balance between too much stimulus and too little stimulation, however. The capacity to absorb discomfort is further growth after the age of sixty-five.

In most cultures, adapting to non-HSP principles becomes difficult for the sensitive person, since most countries favor aggressive behavior. The adaptation of the HSP is based on the society they were born in. A survey of children in Canadian and Chinese schools showed that highly sensitive children in Canada were the least loved and respected, whereas sensitive children in China were the most common. I had a Thailand foreign-exchange student who stayed with me for one year. James was a quiet, gentle sixteen-year-old boy when he came to the USA. He says that compassion and gentleness were respected by the Thais.

Most citizens in Thailand talk and move quietly, and are perhaps the world's gentlest. As I heard him interacting with his Thai buddies, they were going to speak in melodic, soft voices. James had a very hard time adjusting to a violent American high school setting, where male strong and bellicose conduct was prized while gentleness and empathy were deemed a weakness. James began to ignore his vulnerability and sought to become more assertive in the non-HSP Western culture to thrive.

Countries vary when it comes to how much pressure their people are subjected to.

One study indicated that the Dutch hold their kids calmer than the Americans, who subject their babies to more stimuli in general. Kids in India are brought up with a lot of stimuli rendering it difficult for the HSP. Only susceptible people in India are becoming more used to experiencing incessant noise, though. There was an interview of a highly sensitive Indian man who had been living in the USA for five years. Ramesh stated that the longer he lived in America, the more he was acculturated to the comparatively quiet atmosphere, and when he visited India, it was challenging for him. Since he was born in an extremely noisy setting, though, he assured me that he gradually adapts to his native country's overstimulation, and after a while, the excessive noise doesn't disturb him so much.

Although HSPs that are born in over-stimulating settings can deal with intense stimulation more quickly, responsive people brought up in less stressful communities have a harder time coping. A highly sensitive American said she participated with both Westerners and Indians on a cultural tour of India and her tale showed how Americans love their quiet space. She said the Indian and American women had slept in two different large rooms on the street.

In one bed all the Indian women slept together in one corner holding each other like a litter of puppies, while in the other room all the American women slept precisely three rows apart. Likewise, if a rural Montana HSP relocated to Manhattan, the strain on her senses would easily overwhelm her. In the opposite case, sensitive individuals who have become used to urban overstimulation may have trouble adjusting to a peaceful rural environment. While I stayed in California's bucolic Sierra Mountains I had a buddy who was visiting me for the weekend working in central San Francisco. He was nervous by the lack of stimulation and he wanted to go to the nearest town, thirty minutes away. One HSP student living in a busy urban neighborhood told me she had trouble sleeping on a recent visit to the country because of the quietness.

SELF-DISCIPLINE ON EMPATHY

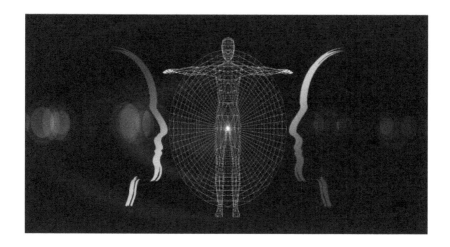

Through knowing, recognizing and appreciating your sensitive nervous system and discovering realistic ways of dealing with your anxiety, you would slowly be able to identify and shed any internalized false beliefs that something is inherently wrong with you. In this culture, HSPs are a large minority that values and thrives on overstimulation, rivalry, and aggression;

However, a compromise has to be found between the non-HSP soldiers and chief executives and the mostly HSP psychologists and artists in order for a society to function at an optimal level.

In reality, if there were more HSPs, we'd probably be living on a safer planet with less conflict, less environmental devastation, and less terrorism. It is the HSP, whose vulnerability helps to create smoke, emissions, and noise restrictions.

However, it is important to note that non-HSPs and rude and insensitive HSPs are very caring and kind. My non-HSP dad was, in truth, one of the most considerate and caring people I ever met.

While most non-HSPs are kindhearted, most cultures exalt the violent characteristics of non-HSPs in the media. Some of the big companies ' non-HSP chief executives severely damaged the earth with indiscriminate oil drilling, clear tree burning, and environmental pollution. The highly sensitive individual has an important mission to act as a counter to the more aggressive behavior of some of the non-HSPs who promote an approach against people, animals, and Mother Nature that is less than compassionate. And though you may have been advised you are too naive, the fact is that the prevalence of cruel ideals has created a world on the brink of disaster, and our only hope of saving the earth is by being compassionate and kind to all sentient beings.

Although our characteristics may be daunting, some of the wonderful benefits of being an HSP may include the following: They are attentive and have the ability to appreciate elegance, fashion, and music profoundly. Thanks to our responsive taste buds, our good sense of smell allows us to thoroughly appreciate sweet, natural scents like roses. They are creative and appear to have a deep experience of the supernatural. We'll note potential hazard, like having a tick creeping on our skin automatically, faster than non-HSPs. We are very mindful of safety issues and will be the first to learn how to evacuate a building in an emergency. We are serious about the animals being treated humanely. We strive to be kind, caring, and patient and render us good advocates, mentors, and healers. They have an enthusiasm for life and, if we are not stressed, will feel love and joy more intensely than non-HSPs.

Some non-HSP society often holds a negative view of our awareness. In all cultures, the HSP is a minority that typically supports the dominant non-HSPs. Non-HSPs can occasionally tell you that something is wrong with you when you show the need for quiet time, or when you feel overwhelmed at work, or when you are taking care of your home duties. It is like discriminating against people based on the color of their skin, ethnicity or national origin to be punished for possessing a finely tuned nervous system. Like other minority groups, it is crucial that we aim to inform the general population regarding our vulnerable nervous system, recognize our vulnerability and find ways to cope with the non-HSP society in the mainstream.

While you don't need to prove it, bring placards that say "Sensitivity Strength!" It would be helpful to discover ways to raise your self-esteem (you really couldn't handle the disruption and discomfort of a presentation anyway). You will increase your self-esteem by reading HSP literature, attending individual therapy or HSP groups or workshops to appreciate the characteristic, and using many of the ideas in this article. Develop new partnerships with other HSPs and seek not to spend time with non-HSP judgmental people who make you feel false. It is also very critical that you don't equate or try to compete with non-HSPs.

High sensitivity in people and understanding

High sensitivity is an innate ability to perceive what comes to HSPs in a very deep, subtle way across our senses. It's not that our eyes and ears are smarter so we figure out more cautiously what goes in. We like to study, analyze, and think. Not even mindful of that operation. We may be mindful of thinking or "ruminating" or "worrying," depending on the mood we're in and the problem we're grappling with, however, more often than not, that occurs without being conscious. We are therefore very intuitive because we tend to know how things turned out to be the way they are and how they play out, but without understanding how we do all of that.

We are also excellent at using subtle signals to figure out what's going on with those that can't communicate through words— animals, insects, children, unconscious pieces of humans, the ill (bodies don't use words), strangers trying to communicate with us, historical people long dead (from our interpretation of their biographies).

HSPs also have close links with our own unconscious, as shown by our vibrant dreams. HSPs will create, through exposure to our desires and body conditions, not only reverence for the unconscious but a wise modesty regarding motives, understanding how much of what we are doing is triggered by unconscious impulses.

Our retrospective inclination always allows us more conscientious — prone to worry, "what if I don't do this?" Or "what if they all do it?" My research finds that we're more concerned about social justice and environmental risks relative to less sensitive people (although perhaps less likely to be active on the political front lines, demanding change). We are also receiving more satisfaction from the arts and from our own life inside. So we tend to think of ourselves as moral, so that, for example, we are on average more willing to sit on a suffering stranger's bedside to give comfort than non-HSPs.

The bad news is that if we pick up on all the subtleties around us, we'll quickly be distracted by high levels of constant, nuanced stimuli as well. It's just a package deal. In today's world, we quickly get overwhelmed.

We are also more sensitive to criticism; we analyze all feedback carefully, including details about our shortcomings. Thanks to traumas, we are also more quickly distressed or nervous, experiencing those more profoundly too.

As a consequence, we can feel less optimism and more fear than those who don't rely as deeply on experiences.

Finally, our susceptibility goes far beyond finer processing of information in the brain, in that we appear to be more responsive to, for example, alcohol, caffeine, sun, cold, itchy textures or other irritants, shifts in the amount of daylight, drugs, and allergens influencing the skin and the sinuses.

IMPORTANCE OF OOPTIMAL AROUSAL LEVEL

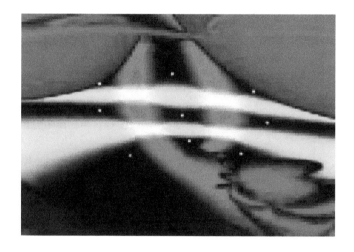

No one performs well or feels good when is over or underaroused (I mean generally arousal here, not physical excitement). This is valid for all species, beginning from conception. When over-stimulated by discomfort, thirst, noise or just a long day, babies scream. And when tiredness is so unstimulated, they scream.

Adults don't like being over-stimulated either — by noise, confusion, discomfort, deadlines, social pressure, terror, rage, sadness, or even too much fun, as when people on holiday can't stand to see one more view, restaurant, or museum. In addition to being physically and psychologically anxious, overarousal may make people feel like they're going to mess up — fail a test, commit an error, have an accident. Everyone is over-dreaded. They also all fear underlying — being idle, impatient, sitting with nothing to do.

Both species like an optimum level of excitement so we humans make adaptations to live there all day— we switch on the radio to raise the enthusiasm, take a nap to decrease it, call a mate to increase it, switching off the television to decrease it, and so on. We're also doing this over longer intervals— changing employment to raise it, preventing divorce to decrease it, traveling overseas to maximize it, heading to the nation to minimize it.

For HSPs the only distinction is that we get overrated a little faster than others. This means that a scenario that excites someone else optimally is too much for us. Yet for them what's good for us can be dull. If our non-HSP partner wants it on we want the radio off. After a long day of exploring we want to linger in our hotel room while our non-HSP mate wants to check out the nightlife. You can see that there is a potential discord.

Does being sensitive equals being an introvert?

Yes and also No. Carl Jung, a psychiatrist, described introversion as a tendency to turn inward, away from worldly things, and choose the abstract realms to think profoundly. This is one of the fundamental aspects of what I mean by sensitivity— its tendency to focus intensely on an event, so that this interpretation is almost more prized than the original object of perception, providing so much rich meaning.

But when most people talk about introversion, they mean social introversion — unlike encountering strangers or socializing in big groups.

Even the Jungian typology tests tend to make the move. Thirty percent of HSPs are not introverts, using this concept (social introversion), and the measures of it. Indeed they are extroverts. So I'll hold to the assumption that the underlying characteristic is not introversion but openness, as most people define it. So, the other socially extroverted HSPs haven't driven away in terms of a misunderstanding.

Why does social introversion nearly describe openness but not quite? I assume 70 percent of HSPs are socially introverted because it's a safe strategy to reduce our stress and spend our time doing what we do best—processing stuff intensely individually or with a close friend, something that you can't usually do with outsiders or in large groups.

However, if HSPs grow up in a society that is normal to groups and others, they are comfortable and even soothing, and these HSPs are extroverts. Similarly, if an HSP grew up being disciplined for being introverted or highly praised for being extroverted, the chosen, common, least insecure type would be extroversion. And plenty of HSPs become extroverts again. It is not born from individual introversion and extroversion itself.

Does being sensitive mean being shy?

There is no reason known that anyone, human or animal, is born shy—that is, fear of being criticized and dismissed on a social level. Like introversion, shyness evolves as one potential response to some of the circumstances of life and does not necessarily characterize the inherited characteristic. Sure, it is harder for HSPs to become nervous and afraid than non-HSPs but only under such conditions. The basic characteristic is awareness. Sensitivity often allows HSPs to stop and scrutinize new situations closely, to note all the subtleties and weigh all their implications. Others misinterpret this pause as terror, or when the circumstance seems to merit it, the pause can transform into a panic.

The distinction between an animal or infant that was born receptive and one that has become timid, nervous, or scared by bad experiences is really quite plain to see. The cautious one just wants to watch and think carefully about a new situation before jumping into it. If you're an outsider, you'll be observed by the kid or the cat, with all the senses tuned to you. Instead, if you're "okay" and don't mimic anyone who's created trouble in the past, it's going to come out, realizing everything about you. You became lifelong friends.

Your appearance will quite confuse the chronically afraid animal or infant, not alertly interested but restlessly, anxiously on watch, not really feeling a lot of details about you. If it ever comes forward, then next time it has to replay the entire process. Quick nobody's a lifelong friend.

A sensitive person who is also scared by past experiences is of necessity very nervous. In fact, research has found consistently that having experienced difficult childhood experiences with one's parents contributes to more shyness in HSPs than it does in non-HSPs. But once again, shyness is the product of maturity and not an inherent essential characteristic. In reality, HSPs with strong infancy have turned out to be less shy than non-HSPs in some of my studies.

Importance of sensitivity

Temperament is the subject of this book but through a HSPs eye. The sensitivity lens is for three reasons: Sensitivity is perhaps the most fundamental inherited trait, its nature influences interactions in particular, and knowledge of this feature is vital to human survival. We shall look one at a time at these three bold claims.

Sensitivity basic

High sensitivity is a common term for the hereditary temperament disparity most commonly studied (known in the past as introversion-extroversion, shyness-boldness, etc.), both in humans and in all the higher species. The subject has a long tradition of study, as it illustrates variations in the nervous system's simple wiring. But that's not the latest term for the feature. In an early step of his research, psychiatrist Carl Jung commented on responsiveness. Psychologist Albert Mehrabian came up with a concept which he named "small scanning" like sensitivity in the 1970s. In 1988 psychiatrist Burton Appleford published "the book Sensitivity—Agony or Ecstasy?"

Appleford thoroughly understood the benefits of that feature, finding it as essential and as subjective as I.Q. In the 1950s child psychologists, Alexander Thomas and Stella Chess identified infant responsiveness as one of nine essential characteristics, and Janet Poland's book on The Sensitive Child published in the same month of 1996 as The Highly Sensitive Person's first printing.

However, sensitivity is far more generally known as a wrong term by many authors hence spreading the wrong message around It has been going under the wrong labels, like shyness, fearfulness, inhibiting, or introversion (as in "that's a nervous puppy" or "he's been born nervous"). Whatever the word for it, it is the most popular differentiation in all societies, after gender and age, created between people, human or animal.

HSPs are very Important to Relationships

The second reason to concentrate on high sensitivity is that it is known that when a partnership involves an HSP it has the ability to be extremely effective or quite disappointing. While we reflect only 20 percent of the population, the probability of a partnership that involves an HSP (if we assume people are paired randomly) is about 36 percent. If we include individuals of low discomfort the percentage is higher. If we include partnerships as well as romantic relationships, will non-HSP obviously try to love any HSP, and definitely any HSP would try to love at least one non-HSP. You could also assume that information regarding sensitivity differences is important to each couple, in that one of them will always be more sensitive than the other.

There are fairly obvious explanations why HSPs are useful in relationships— for starters, they are attentive, sensitive, mindful of the moods of others, and willing to think deeply about what is going on.

There are many explanations why HSPs can also be lousy mates, none of them incurable. But they all are subjects for this novel. For starters, because HSPs hit overload earlier than others, we can either try to ignore it, which is deadly for us and sure to build up our resentment, or we have to thwart some of the wishes of our spouse, building up their resentment. HSPs may have an uncommon fear of intimacy as well as confrontation. And in a series of carefully designed research studies, it's been found that HSPs growing up in unstable, dysfunctional communities are more likely than non-HSPs to have the traits that other research has considered most risky for relationships: pessimism, low self-esteem, depression, insecurity, and a weak attachment style.

Without those stressors, HSPs are not more prone to have these traits than others. By distinguishing the consequences of personal history from personality, we can provide better attention to both problems, rendering each less daunting.

Sensitivity has a crucial role to play concerning human life

The essential requirement of two breeds

Biologists once believed that each species evolved towards some kind of single ideal form, ideally suited to their climate. The ideal shifted if the environment changed, or the organisms became extinct.

Yet considering the hypothesis, it turns out that most animals have found a better solution for their life: two (or more) perfect forms, two methods of survival. When one species "breed" is unable to handle things, the other may well do better.

The two temperaments that I term sensitivity and nonsensitivity are assumed to fulfill precisely the clever survival plan. Sensitive people gather more details before they act, carefully check stuff out, and take fewer impulsive chances. Those without the characteristic are taking more risks. The HSP operates by the adages "think before you run" and "a stitch in time saves nine." The non-HSP is motivated by "he who hesitates is defeated" and "opportunity just knocks once." All strategies to life work, though in some cases one will be an asset, in others.

Several species — primates, pigs, goats, rabbits, and elk, to name a few—consider this variation in tactics. It potentially exists in all the higher animals. Some pumpkinseed sunfish join traps set in ponds as one example, and others do not. The two sunfish forms vary not only in this behavior but also in the activities of spawning, foraging, and predator avoidance. They even have numerous parasites. I was advised that when California Fish and Game experts do a deer census by setting up cameras with trip wires that the deer crosses in the night, about 20 percent (the responsive ones, I presume) would skip such trip wires so that the amount of deer must be applied to the census automatically.

Every Culture Favors One Breed Over the Other

Getting a certain number of vigilant, alert-to-the-subtle individuals within a given group makes sense for social animals such as humans.

They are the ones who first fear that the bushes hold lions. Then it is the nonsensitive people that run in anxiously to scare the lions clear. But most people are more likely to favor one over the other. Immigrant cultures, or those who prefer or need an extreme survival strategy, tend to favor the risk-takers. Societies living close to the planet value their most sensitive herbalists, trackers, and shamans, and many traditional, highly educated, prosperous cultures value their most sensitive rulers, priests, historians, healers, visionaries, musicians, physicists, academics, and counselors.

Non-HSPs are favored in an offensive society, and that fact will become apparent everywhere. Even in the pumpkinseed sunfish analysis mentioned above, the U.S. biologists who wrote the article identified the sunfish who went into the traps as the "strong" fish who acted "normally," while the others were "shy," but were the untrapped fish always shy? Why not smuggle? After all, one could identify them as simply as the smart sunfish, and the others as dumb ones. No one knew what the sunfish thought but the researchers were positive because they had been trained to be by their family. Those who delay are terrified; those who are not natural.

Here's a good study to remember: this studies as mentioned earlier compared primary school children in Shanghai with those in Canada showed that smart, silent children in China were among the most esteemed by their peers, and in Canada, they were among the least valued. HSPs that grow up in communities where they are not accepted must be influenced by that lack of respect.

HSPs importance is greater in aggressive cultures

Although societies generally prefer one characteristic a little more than the other, when this goes too far it becomes risky, as is the case with many of Western culture, which continues to pay heavily for its overvaluation of impulsive violence. One important historical explanation for this overvaluation is that all Western (and some Eastern) societies are descended from a small group of strong, nomadic people who came from Europe-Asia steppes. They existed by invasion, capturing the herds of other men, and ultimately most of the world, becoming the basis of, among others, the Greeks, Romans, Gauls, Germanic tribes, and India's upper castes— thus they are called the Indo-Europeans.

Anthropologists also found that afterward, Indo-European culture and every culture to rise from the steppes, and most violent civilizations in general (such as the Aztecs), have two ruling classes: the warrior kings and the priestly advisors. Kings of soldiers are the impulsive masters of raids and nation builders. Our high-powered corporate, financial, and military leaders are equal today. The priestly advisors— usually, I believe, HSPs — are again the students, the healers, the jurors, the historians, the musicians, etc. They guide the kingdoms of fighters.

An HSP may even be the president of a nation — consider Lincoln, an HSP who perfectly balanced the generals of its warrior-king Civil War.

The role of the priestly counselor is to see that the kings of warriors are thinking a little about the consequences of their actions— for example, starting a war that they cannot fight, or that will do more harm than good. If the strength between these two parties is shared (as in the executive and the government branch of the judiciary), then everything is going well. However, the priestly advisors, normally we HSPs, have to demonstrate themselves for this balance to occur.

We have to respect ourselves and our kind of power and influence in order to do that.

Getting Back to Balance, and How Relationships Can Help

But, instead of expressing ourselves, we HSPs have been losing influence in the last fifty years. This is not due to some plot but merely because our conventional fields seem to have evolved, requiring the kind of individuals who can excel under intense pressure and stress levels. Such fields currently need more than ever HSPs in them. Everyone can see the negative consequences of less compassionate physicians, patients, attorneys, teachers, and artists being there.

Everyone also loses in business and government as representatives with nervous systems which are not likely to represent make impulsive, violent decisions for the rest of us. Some of those choices will impact our very life here in particular. I'm sure, for example, that HSPs are far more worried about climate change than non-HSPs. A population that does not take advantage of both of its "breeds" or forms poses a serious drawback for itself.

As you go through this book, focusing on your loving relationships, you don't just support yourself and those who are dear to you.

Often, your partnerships help you carry out your vital role in the world.

Firstly, you have a direct influence on those you respect, and they echo your beliefs to others in exchange. But more significantly, they will give you the trust, encouragement, and experience that you need to be a force among a wider group of individuals. Finally, while this may not extend to you directly, the more closely related HSPs, the more HSPs there will be that have children or grow or affect others ' children.

Making a point of it all

It may be time to offer a model for you. The book incorporates a variety of universal terms such as disposition, attitude, and gender, including individual characteristics such as vulnerability, feel-seeking, introversion, extroversion, and shyness, and soon to come, avoidance of touch, relationship style, depression, anxiety, and sexual activity desires, just to list a couple. How will they come in?

I like to say that our personalities are three-level. On the ground floor, we consider the simple circuitry, what I call inherited personality. Sensitivity and the desire for pleasure are maybe the main indicators, along with energy level, general intellect, and some unique talents. Such bottom-floor temperamental characteristics permeate the nervous system, affecting everything from how quickly you startle and how often societal injustices bother you.

We're discovering attitude characteristics on the second landing. Personality is the lasting component, painting or aromatizing much of the habits.

Personality emerges from the association of the first-floor personality with external factors and personal history— it is how your hereditary disposition across your social and personal interactions has worked out for you in a particular way. Traits of personality include introversion, extroversion, confidence, pessimism, type of relationship, willingness or avoidance of touch, shyness and so on. As we have shown, HSPs appear to be introverts because they have noticed that it prevents them from over-stimulation from personal interactions. HSPs feel nervous because they've had distressing social interactions. Cultures add to the temperament by finding things a bit more natural and desirable than most to get these characteristics. Extroversion, for example, is preferred in the U.S., Australia, and Israel but is not so necessary in Japan, Sweden, or Tibet.

In the United States imagination is strongly regarded but not so important in India.

Lastly, the third floor contains the obvious attitudes, behaviors, and interests that endure for at least a period but not as often as personality characteristics. Reasons include daily workouts, heading to parties every night, procrastinating, making multiple intimate relations, consuming coffee every morning, or being involved with voluntary contributions. Such habits alter more quickly and regularly, but not always, as each is always a result of the floors under them.

The inherited fundamental characteristics of the first floor are both more and less prominent than those of the second and third floors — more because they are the essential cabling, less important because they are just the context for social and personal interaction. We also seem to neglect social and particularly cultural interactions as they are much the same for anyone in a single culture; like the air we breathe, we don't consider our own environment until we get to know a Zulu or an Inuit well.

Final thoughts

You've come to better understand your vulnerability. But it takes time to work the awareness in your mind deep down. Changing these views takes time to reflect, alone, and then time to talk to those you respect about your current point of view and even disagree with them about the proposals. Yet, also be careful. Hang on with the operation.

Changing your temperamental biases – i.e. temperamental? Xenophobia? – always takes time to be sensitive to external forces that threaten your self-respect and others. For one, certain behaviors in a violent society that are less than desirable are easily pathologized.

We learn that he has a social phobia, that she is obsessive-compulsive, that he's codependent, that she's a suicidal guy. It is about a degree, isn't it? In addition, less appreciated disparities sometimes transform into problems merely because those with them will indeed face more social rejection.

But from a temperamental viewpoint, such presumed pathologies can only be the product of normal variation that induces some of us to retreat to minimize stress, to be tidy, to avoid repercussions, to be sensitive to the needs of others, or to feel the tragedy of human condition.

If we do not accept natural personality differences, and therefore do not value them, we seek to mold and change ourselves or our spouses, to become more "standard" (actually, more like the model of culture). In our society, "natural" (ideal) people are happy, friendly, confident, success-oriented, and autonomous. We assume it is our privilege to be like that or to have such a friend or partner. Variations from the standard are actually more common than the norm, and they are very good in their own way.

Then there are the variations, the subject of the next essay, which are not deemed suitable for a particular gender. Men should be firm, stoical, rational, and not really reactive. Women should be gregarious, good with children, skillful in expressing feelings, and profoundly intuitive. This indicates you've been shortchanged if you don't have a "real man" or "feminine woman" for a mate. It's time to work on that— sensitivity and identity have been misunderstood for too long.

FIND YOURSELF AND FORGETTING STEROTYPES (EMPATH HEALING)

The aim of this chapter is to save and preserve your love— the person you love, your feelings of love in general — from the consequences of the harmful gender stereotypes can do. Rigid assumptions and biases of class cause trouble for all, but more difficult for HSPs. We suit less with the assumptions and struggle more from all the impacts of the biases. As a consequence, with the other group, we can have different problems-mistrust, fear of rejection, misunderstandings. These must be discussed in this book before moving any further.

However, we choose to concentrate on the relationship between men and women for obvious reasons. For most men, this is where identity differences rear their most latent, ugliest eyes. Moreover, these sorts of same-sex relationships, which are the nearest marriages for some of you, are just as rooted in a culture where gender is the "great divide." Therefore, with a little change, everything said here can also be beneficial for same-sex relationships.

Reasons highly sensitive people feel uneasy amongst other people

The animal kingdom is split into male and female, and people are split into men and women, and this concept has made a tangle of problems and some pleasure too. Each wants the other and has dreams of the other—both for biological reasons and for a long-term relationship's enjoyment, health, and anticipation. Sometimes, though, standing in the way of that connection is misogyny.

Cultural Reasons

In our society, a woman feels forced to be sexually attractive to men in order to examine this annoying problem. It goes without saying that she is always advised to support herself and reach her own objectives. Attracting an individual nevertheless remains a discreet goal. When everything goes right, a woman succeeds in that, and the two admire her beauty, as well as her many successes, and accept the changes in her image as she ages. But often the attractiveness of a young woman appears insignificant to her, attracts the wrong kind of attention, is her only currency in the world, or "fades." Meanwhile, people seem overwhelmingly respected for their successes and are able to find women in their existence. While women feel unfairly treated, or fail to be victims— with great strenuousness — or become dismissive, or "masculine." Through all this, women grow men's conscious or unconscious mistrust.

Meanwhile, a boy grows up trying to act in control, to become a "real man." At the same time, he waits patiently and sensitively to grasp what the hopelessly vague, indirect, nonsensical manifestations of women's needs seem to be. Which happens to be very different from his perception of the issue. He feels unjustly punished for the consequences of a society he failed to create, and for a few men's blatant sexism and abuse.

In HSPs, the challenges of each class are amplified, partially because we are so much more conscious of the subtleties behind those tales.

BIOLOGICAL STRANGENESS

According to Jungian scholar Polly Young-Eisendrath, our basic differences go back to the roots of each gender's mistrust of the other—men can never be women, women can also never be men. Each is always an outsider to the other, a "stranger." During infancy, we know that the two groups are exclusive clubs, and rumors begin in our own club about what's going on in the other— rumors that are, of course, compounded by the racism in our society. When we grow we have our own specific images of the Others that we have come to hate and love. In the words of Young-Eisendrath, "They may be angels or devils, seductive or celibate, but they have enormous power because of their perceived disparity. As adolescents, we... place one or more [of these pictures] on people of the opposite sex for a variety of reasons— to protect ourselves, to fall in love, to accuse another... These [pictures] prowl through our evenings and capture us inadvertently during the day. With all these explanations for anxiety, mistrust and anticipation, when we are alone with the other group, we can be quite nervous about what will happen."

Not Feeling Like the "Ideal" of Manhood or Womanhood

We may also greatly impact our stress with the other group by not thinking like the "ideal" man or woman. Never mind the reality that HSPs are born as many boys as girls— if you are a guy you shouldn't be sensitive. Sure, the "weak guy" has a new interest but mainly as a source of jokes.

You can be responsive when you're a woman, particularly to the needs and desires of others. In reality, you would have been born receptive in this way, more involved in interacting around others and perfecting your beauty, even though you are in reality profoundly introverted or enjoy your job rather than socializing or caring. Therefore, you will not be so reactive as to need some downtime. "I am a woman; I am strong." In brief, desirable women are ambitious, agile and powerful in a non-HSP manner, in this society. And in reality, as with people, responsiveness is at odds with the image of women in our society.

This feeling that, in infancy, we are not the definition of manhood or womanhood starts. Studies have shown that mothers sometimes identify a timid daughter as their favorite child–typically a misnomer for being extremely responsive. Yet there's a price for this favoritism: these girls are frequently over-protected and tend to feel isolated and less capable than other children. In the meanwhile, mothers sometimes define a "shy" son as their least favorite, loving such boys practically less. Ouch. Ouch. Such mothers may not intend to be discriminatory against their own children but they are unconsciously influenced by their society to see a gentle boy as not the ideal.

If mothers overprotect vulnerable children, these girls grow up thinking they will still require that overprotection— the security of a man later— and would happily give up their power for it. Responsive daughters, less valued by their mothers, grow up wanting us to care less because they can cover their vulnerability somewhere. In brief, all genders ' HSPs will grow up with a sense of trust and skepticism as men and women, both of which damages their capacity, to be honest toward the other sex.

HOW DIFFERENT ARE WE REALLY?

Having reviewed data from many separate surveys I conducted, I noticed no significant variations in their relationship performance or happiness between highly sensitive women (HSWs) and non-HSWs, or between highly sensitive men (HSMs) and non-HSMs. The possible unique concerns that would be addressed are not intended to suggest that collectively we have more challenges than our gender non-HSPs. Yet suppose, the problems they have are very special.

Luckily, one of the main advantages for HSPs living in our high-pressure society is that it is constantly empowering men and women to do whatever they do best — what counts is who gets the work done, not holding conventional gender stereotypes intact. That should offer more freedom for HSPs to express their specific personalities. Nevertheless, because humans tend to generalize — like men are better at this, women are better at that — we can propose the half-faced alternative of providing four genders: HSWs, HSMs, non-HSWs, and non-HSMs. (Add High sensitive seekers (HSS) to the mix and you get eight) The structure makes us completely special!

Four genders offer us double the number of socially limited forms of life, twice the amount of equality and versatility.

More seriously, we'll continue by looking separately at the challenges of HSWs and HSMs, but we highly recommend that you learn about each other.

HSWs and HSMs are admirably close. And before this chapter finishes, we'll explore ways to heal both HSMs and HSWs from the effects of gender prejudice.

How Gender Prejudices Damage Relationships for Highly Sensitive Women (HSW)

Sensitive or not, women have a more challenging time in life — research suggests that they are more influenced by turbulent childhoods, have poorer self-esteem, have difficulty standing up in college and gaining power, lack their skills, are compensated less for the same job, are much more likely to remain in poverty in their elderly age, and so on. The explanations for that are clear. Yeah, progress is happening and wounds are healing gradually, generation after generation.

A less sensitive woman with more feminine experience may have only went out after college on her own, or after a couple of years of this kind of marriage, and studied how to do it by trial and error. Yet it can appear daunting to an HSW, instant, disputed freedom. Furthermore, all the individuality, advocacy, rage, and community practices encouraged by feminism seem personally dangerous and, as an HSP, you need to pause and focus on the hazards before taking risks, particularly if you lack your family's help.

You might also have become more influenced by misogyny as, as an HSW, you are forced to take up and analyze more carefully all the derogatory signals that often hit you regarding women— whether in patriarchal words, in the usage of women's bodies to market goods, in unequal care at school or at college, or in trying to be vigilant such that you are not assaulted or seem to be willing to be assaulted. If for the other discrepancy, the vulnerability, you've always learned to feel bad for yourself, you bear two motives to feel less than good and to love, or dislike the first naive man approaching you. Sexism destroys one's ability to care, to say the obvious.

Having a dismissive or absent father

HSPs-both men and women are strongly influenced by how our fathers were interested in our development. This makes sense because fathers have historically been concerned with moving out there and bringing it into the community, right or wrong. Fathers are also the ones to give certain abilities to make it. And three cheers to everyone that did.

Fathers, though, appear to teach females fewer of those abilities. An absent and insensitive father not only do they not tell them how to live in the society, but the HSWs harshness could force her to center her life on satisfying and placating — something that HSPs would do so quickly anyway. In the meantime, mother's role-modeling that women have little choice but to depend on people like her father.

However, even the best-intentioned fathers still mistake encouraging their delicate daughters to escape obstacles. Perhaps they maintain the traditional (patriarchal) view that females should be sheltered; carry and raise children primarily; be more frail, fragile, and reliant on others; and be prevented from experiencing life and perhaps being sexually "taken advantage of." And it may appear to her father that a vulnerable daughter is uniquely suitable (or doomed) to rely on men all of her life. A father once advised his son when he was a kid that he would be better off not attending my brother's math classes — you could be so brilliant that no one would want you. He didn't inform my less responsive sister too much.

As an HSP, you thoroughly analyzed both the guidance and the overarching concern regarding marginalized women.

In comparison to your reaction about being alone in the universe, your father has essentially defined your thoughts towards people in general and how you believe they should feel toward you. When your father has been unavailable, disrespectful, or not involved in teaching you skills, you may mistakenly conclude that you have been unattractive or dull to him. Once, if you were still feeling weak for being emotional, you were influenced even more.

So, you had come to perceive all people to be uninteresting and unattractive.

You can feel nervous and overburden in the company of people in expectation of rejection. You can tend to question your attraction even in a partnership, or even your partner's worth (because he's attracted to you, and you don't trust yourself).

Another issue that may emerge with fathers is that so much of the wrong kind of sexual attention may persuade any woman, particularly an HSW, that her sexuality is the only thing she has to offer the universe, and that she does not have any option to hand it up.

Sexual victimization

Rape, incest sexual harassment— we've just heard about it so much that we're sick of it but it doesn't take away the impact on your mind or on how you feel about people. Once, HSWs are usually more vigilant of potential hazards (even more so once we have encountered a first-hand hazard) and can generally feel less comfortable in the environment.

Therefore our lives can be heavily dominated by the influence of the violent male attacker and the potentially violent male within every guy we meet— the aspect of a man who believed, even if he denied it, that he is entitled to a woman's body or that women "really want it, and when they say no, they mean yes." Remove the consequences of any actual sexual assault which is nothing less than soul-destroying, and an HSW can find trusting, joyful sexual relationships with men all but impossible without much healing work.

Going back and forth with men

As an HSW, you grew up understanding that much of this discrimination was internalized by men too, and that they certainly gained from the superior position they were granted. One answer was to win over people, charm them into sharing their influence or resources, having you be their servants or their sidekicks. On the other side, when you knew that you were sacrificing yourself for a tiny portion of the wealth that would have been sharing with you all along, you were undoubtedly still defiant. You didn't want anyone to believe. You may have also spoken about dominance towards us. Yet you as fellow human beings also have respect towards men; none of this is necessarily their responsibility. Back and forth — how are they to feel? Everything you conclude appears to be false, and yet other people do the same, which will cause you to distrust men and women alike.

You're not sure whether to act, or even how you're going to respond at the moment, even less how it's going to work, you're more curious for people (in the non-sexual sense), less clearheaded. As an HSP, all the stress and anticipation will cause you to want to completely escape guys. But ignoring them makes them much more of a "strange type" and potentially harmful to your well-being, so you in their presence become more uncomfortable so overbearing.

CONCLUSION

Thank you for reading all this book!

It was amazing for men and women. Women say, "Men are mean, cruel brutes," as if they never were people like this. Men say, "Women are crazy, greedy, and controlling men only," as if men never are like that. Only so long will we hate, revile and banish one another. Now is the time to understand that we are actually afraid, reviling, and banishing the other half of us. And HSPs ought first to be able to see that fact. Counseling or psychotherapy may help the HSP deal with the pressures of life in a non-HSP environment that is overstimulating. You might want to see a professional psychologist, a certified marriage and family specialist, or a social worker qualified. When you can't afford to pay for private therapy appointments, nearly every area has low-cost rehabilitation facilities (check the phone book for the mental health department in your city or county). You might also want to take part in a positive group therapy program.

How do treatment and psychotherapy differ? Maybe you speak of them as a spectrum. At the conclusion of the session, you will receive information, advice, and tips to implement what you have learned in this book. Nonetheless, you need to operate from the continuum's end in psychotherapy whether you have persistent unhealthy feelings (depression, fear, anger) that conflict with your existence if you have been unable to submit advice for treatment.

HSPs are particularly afraid of intimacy, I believe we are far more likely to want intimacy than others on average and drive others towards it, especially if we are comfortable, either "given" or through good parenting.

You have already taken a step towards your improvement.

Best wishes!

CPSIA information can be obtained
at www.ICGtesting.com
Printed in the USA
BVHW092152080621
609009BV00008B/926

9 781802 165845